D1131173

OCEAN LIFE UP CLOSE

Parrotfish

by Mari Schuh

BLASTOFF! READERS 3

BELLWETHER MEDIA • MINNEAPOLIS, MN

Note to Librarians, Teachers, and Parents:

Blastoff! Readers are carefully developed by literacy experts and combine standards-based content with developmentally appropriate text.

Level 1 provides the most support through repetition of high-frequency words, light text, predictable sentence patterns, and strong visual support.

Level 2 offers early readers a bit more challenge through varied simple sentences, increased text load, and less repetition of high-frequency words.

Level 3 advances early-fluent readers toward fluency through increased text and concept load, less reliance on visuals, longer sentences, and more literary language.

Level 4 builds reading stamina by providing more text per page, increased use of punctuation, greater variation in sentence patterns, and increasingly challenging vocabulary.

Level 5 encourages children to move from "learning to read" to "reading to learn" by providing even more text, varied writing styles, and less familiar topics.

Whichever book is right for your reader, Blastoff! Readers are the perfect books to build confidence and encourage a love of reading that will last a lifetime!

This edition first published in 2017 by Bellwether Media, Inc.

No part of this publication may be reproduced in whole or in part without written permission of the publisher. For information regarding permission, write to Bellwether Media, Inc., Attention: Permissions Department, 5357 Penn Avenue South, Minneapolis, MN 55419.

Library of Congress Cataloging-in-Publication Data

Names: Schuh, Mari C., 1975- , author.
Title: Parrotfish / by Mari Schuh.
Description: Minneapolis, MN : Bellwether Media, Inc., 2017. | Series: Blastoff! Readers. Ocean Life Up Close | Includes bibliographical references and index. | Audience: Ages 5 to 8. | Audience: Grades K to 3.
Identifiers: LCCN 2016034523 (print) | LCCN 2016044218 (ebook) | ISBN 9781626175716 (hardcover : alk. paper) | ISBN 9781681032924 (ebook)
Subjects: LCSH: Parrotfishes–Juvenile literature.
Classification: LCC QL638.S3 S346 2017 (print) | LCC QL638.S3 (ebook) | DDC 597/.7–dc23
LC record available at https://lccn.loc.gov/2016034523

Editor: Christina Leighton   Designer: Brittany McIntosh

Printed in the United States of America, North Mankato, MN.

Table of Contents

rusty
parrotfish

Parrotfish are colorful fish with large scales. Many are red, green, blue, and yellow.

These fish live in shallow water. About 80 types of parrotfish swim in the world's **coral reefs**.

bullethead
parrotfish

Parrotfish come in many sizes. Some are just 4 inches (10 centimeters) long.

Parrotfish Sizes

Smallest
bluetip
parrotfish

average
human

4 inches
(10 centimeters) long

Largest
bumphead
parrotfish

average
human

4 feet
(1.2 meters) long

bumphead
parrotfish

bluetip
parrotfish

Others grow up to 4 feet (1.2 meters) long. A bumphead parrotfish can weigh 101 pounds (46 kilograms)!

Parrotfish get their name from their teeth. The teeth join together to look like a parrot's beak.

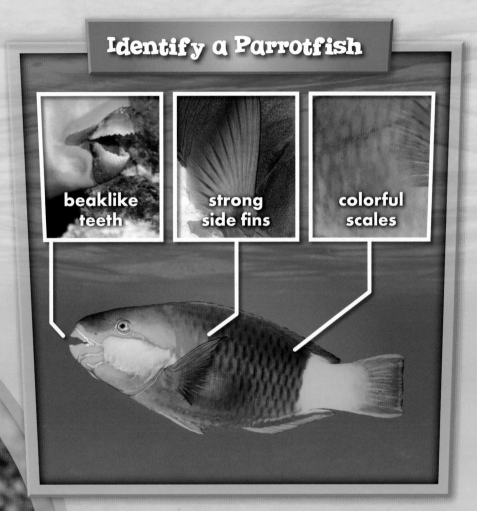

Identify a Parrotfish

beaklike teeth

strong side fins

colorful scales

These fish swim with their strong side fins. They use them like oars. Most other fish move forward with their tails.

Parrotfish use their teeth to bite off chunks of **coral**. Most parrotfish only want the **algae** in the coral.

Teeth in their throats crush the coral into tiny pieces. Parrotfish bodies turn the coral into sand.

turtle grass

green algae

cauliflower corals

Singapore parrotfish

11

Day and Night

Parrotfish are active during the day. They often swim in groups called **schools**.

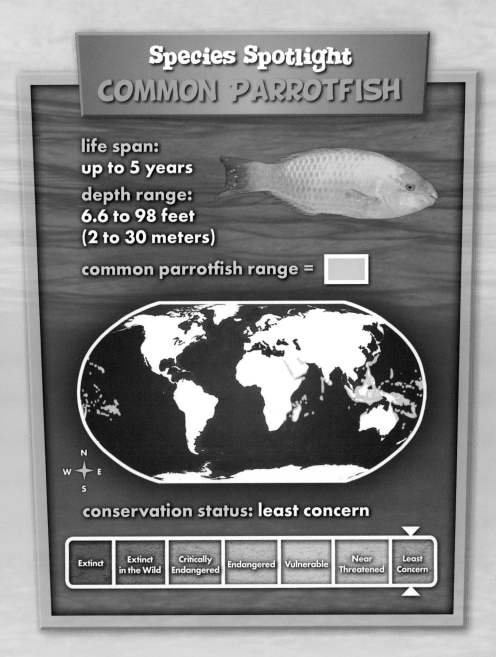

Species Spotlight
COMMON PARROTFISH

life span:
up to 5 years

depth range:
6.6 to 98 feet
(2 to 30 meters)

common parrotfish range =

conservation status: **least concern**

Extinct	Extinct in the Wild	Critically Endangered	Endangered	Vulnerable	Near Threatened	Least Concern

Some schools have only four or five parrotfish. Others can have more than 40 parrotfish!

purplestreak parrotfish

At night, parrotfish sleep alone in holes or cracks. They also **burrow** into the sand.

Some parrotfish make a layer of **mucus** to cover their bodies. The mucus helps keep them safe from **parasites**.

Parrotfish have a few other ways to avoid **predators**. Their mucus may hide their scent at night.

Their colors can act as **camouflage**. They blend in with the coral reef.

blue-barred parrotfish

Sea Enemies

whitetip reef sharks

spotted moray eels

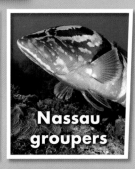
Nassau groupers

redband parrotfish

Growing Big and Bright

yellowband
parrotfish

Parrotfish change their colors and patterns over time. Young parrotfish have dull colors.

As they grow up, their colors become brighter. The bright colors help parrotfish find mates.

red-speckled parrotfish

Female parrotfish release thousands of eggs in shallow water. The babies **hatch** about a day later.

Then the young swim around the coral reef and find food. Soon, they will get bigger and brighter!

Glossary

algae—plants and plantlike living things; most kinds of algae grow in water.

burrow—to dig a hole or tunnel

camouflage—a way of using color to blend in with surroundings

coral—a hard material formed from the skeletons of small animals

coral reefs—structures made of coral that usually grow in shallow seawater

hatch—to break out of an egg

mucus—a clear liquid that covers the bodies of some parrotfish

parasites—living things that survive on or in other living things; parasites offer nothing for the food and protection they receive.

predators—animals that hunt other animals for food

schools—groups of parrotfish

To Learn More

AT THE LIBRARY

Hansen, Grace. *Tropical Fish*. Minneapolis, Minn.: Abdo Kids, 2015.

Schuetz, Kari. *Life in a Coral Reef*. Minneapolis, Minn.: Bellwether Media, 2016.

Schuh, Mari. *Corals*. Minneapolis, Minn.: Bellwether Media, 2017.

ON THE WEB

Learning more about parrotfish is as easy as 1, 2, 3.

1. Go to www.factsurfer.com.

2. Enter "parrotfish" into the search box.

3. Click the "Surf" button and you will see a list of related web sites.

With factsurfer.com, finding more information is just a click away.

Index

The images in this book are reproduced through the courtesy of: Rich Carey, front cover, pp. 3, 4, 5;
WaterFrame/ Alamy, pp. 7 (top), 20; Williams, J. T./ Carpenter, K. E./ Van Tassell, J. L./ Hoetjes, P./ Toller,
W./ Etnoyer, P./ Smith, M./ Wikipedia, p. 7 (bottom); Ingram Publishing/ SuperStock, p. 8; Zainal Amar
Zainal Abidin, p. 9 (top left); Jolanta Wojcicka, p. 9 (top center); serg_dibrova, p. 9 (top right, bottom); James
St. John/ Wikipedia, p. 11 (top left); Aleksandar Mijatovic, p. 11 (top center); Seaphotoart, p. 11 (top right);
Georgie Holland/ Age Fotostock/ SuperStock, p. 11 (bottom); Tobias Friedrich/ F1 ONLINE/ SuperStock,
p. 12; Feathercollector, p. 13; metha1819, p. 14; LOOK-foto/ SuperStock, p. 15; Leonardo Gonzalez, p. 16;
aquapix, p. 17 (top left); Debra James, p. 17 (top center); Yann hubert, p. 17 (top right); Universal Images
Group/ SuperStock, p. 17 (bottom); FLPA/ SuperStock, p. 18; OceanwideImages.com/ Ocean Wide Images,
p. 19; Ethan Daniels/ Alamy, p. 21.

city would not be sufficient by itself to influence a plant-location decision, but it is an attractive added inducement.

A special opportunity for an export industry exists for Toroid that was not available at Columbia. The heaviest single component of capital investment in a city is the private housing sector. If we assume that approximately $5000 per person is required for housing, a total investment of $5 billion is involved. It is important for the success of Toroid that the cost of housing be reduced; this will be an important inducement for immigration. One way of reducing the cost of housing is the use of industrialized mass production techniques. To date, industrialized housing has failed to live up to its potential in the United States because of the absence of a concentrated market. If, however, we were able to guarantee a minimum market of 10,000 units and annual sales in excess of $100 million over a period of more than a decade, this would provide a powerful inducement to an industrialized housing enterprise. After sharpening their production skills on the captive market in Toroid, the housing manufacturers could begin supplying the regional market, thus providing Toroid's first export industry. Home appliance manufacturers likewise would be interested, and as the labor pool develops, other industry should also be attracted.

Industrialized housing has many critics. Peter Blake, an architect writing in the *Atlantic Monthly,* is one of them.[5] But Blake seems to have trouble distinguishing cause from effect. He tells us that the reason the U.S. housing industry is in trouble "is that nobody except mortgage bankers can afford to buy or rent the new houses or apartments we are building." No doubt this is true, but the statement seems similar to that of the physician who claimed the patient died because of his failure to continue breathing. Blake's second reason for the housing industry's failure is its supposed concentration on industrialized mass production techniques despite the vanishingly small share of the market held by mass production builders.

Yet *something* is wrong, or the mass production builders would be thriving. Studies[6] indicate that several important factors are involved.

- *Lack of quality control.* Rather than implying higher quality than conventional stick-built construction, "prefabricated home" is a term of approbation.
- *Lack of uniform building codes.* Building codes vary from county to county with no discernible logic. This requires the manufacturer either to vary his production standards or to build to the most stringent code, thus raising costs.
- *Transport costs.* These are not the major problem. Wentz[6] quotes

costs of approximately $1 per mile, which add less than $1000 to the purchase price.

- *Lack of cost advantage.* Even National Homes, the country's largest manufacturer, is operating well below its estimated minimum effective production rate.
- *Lack of adequate funding.* Most industrialized manufacturers are either underfinanced or badly managed or both. They compete against individual craft builders who can exhibit large pricing elasticity for a short period if pressed.
- *Lack of brand recognition.* Because quality control has been poor in industrialized housing, any brand recognition that exists is probably a deterrent in marketing the unit.

All of these problems can be overcome by business practices that have been standard in most industries for years. One must admit a momentary tinge of admiration for the flamboyant, individualistic buccaneers of the housing business as they ran rings around Weyerhauser, General Electric, and the conglomerates who thought they saw a special profit opportunity in housing in the 1960s but who ended deep in red ink. Yet rationalization must come to the housing business and come rapidly. Already the cost of housing has escalated to the point where the average new home constructed is priced well beyond the ability to pay of the average wage earner.[7]

10.8 Energy and Toroid

A number of large-block users of energy in the United States, such as colleges, commercial concerns, and industries, have reported a tripling of their energy bills in the recent past. Many home owners notice a doubling in fuel costs and even larger increases in electric bills, and gasoline has more than doubled in price. Energy policy has become a matter of national political concern.[8] In our forward planning of Toroid we need not concern ourselves with the energy problem in detail. Rather, we must answer only a few general questions. It will be possible to derive, from these, guidelines upon which design decisions can be based. The two must important questions to be answered are the following.

Is the recent rise in energy costs a temporary one brought on, perhaps, by political maneuvering, or must it be considered permanent? The short answer to this question appears to be that the present high price of energy is permanent. One could argue that the oil embargo and the sharp increase in oil prices imposed by the OPEC nations during the 1973 Arab–Israeli war could have been avoided, but a long-term trend toward increasingly scarce and increasingly expensive fossil fuels had been evident for years before that event. Only widespread usage of nuclear power could serve to lower the cost of energy, which brings us to the second question.

Will cheap, plentiful nuclear energy be available for Toroid? We must answer "no" for the short term. Wide-spread use of conventional boiling-water reactors certainly seems to be a reasonable projection. Environmental and safety concerns have slowed the already snail-like licensing process, but conventional reactors will continue to be installed. Nevertheless, the cost of such reactors has increased so significantly that a decrease in the price of electricity produced by them is not to be expected. Significant energy cost reductions have been promised with the introduction of the breeder reactor. Unfortunately, this device has proved to be considerably more difficult and more expensive to develop than was expected only a few years ago. Thus the breeder is not a high probability for commercial introduction in the next 10 years, and Toroid will be designed around a conventional reactor. Should the conventional nuclear reactor be withdrawn from commercial use, which we deem unlikely, and fossil fuels be the only alternative, then energy will be still more expensive. Thus our position estimate is conservative.

A number of implications of expensive energy seem reasonable.

- A trend toward a more compact organization of the urban environment will develop.
- Smaller private automobiles will become the rule and will more and more be used for leisure and recreational activities. Objections to mass transit for the journey to work will markedly decrease. Multiple-car families will reduce the number of cars they own, but the private automobile will not disappear.
- Home architectural design will begin to consider energy conservation. Window placement, sunshades, cross ventilation, insulation, and other "natural" methods of heating and cooling will become more popular. Electric heating will become rare, and the growth in home air conditioning will slow.
- Home appliances will be marketed and purchased with an eye to their energy consumption. Lower home temperatures in the winter will be more common, and these, in turn, will have an influence on clothing fashions.
- Industries will reexamine the processes of production in order to make them more energy efficient or to substitute other processes that will become commercially attractive because of increased energy costs.
- Research and development on methods for producing clean energy from coal will boom.
- Other.

By examining the current energy balance sheets for U. S. cities with a population of 1 million, we should be able to identify the sectors that promise an important reduction in total comsumption.[9] Table 10.1 provides such an estimate. Substantial reductions, up to 20 percent perhaps,

Table 10.1   *Estimated Annual Energy Demand By Sector in a U. S. City of 1 Million People in a Moderate Climate* (SOURCE: Miller, *loc. cit.*)

Sector	Annual Consumption (10^9 kWh/yr)		· Proportion
Industrial production		56.0	44.8
Transportation		31.2	24.9
Residential		24.0	19.1
Heating	14.5		
Appliances	7.3		
Cooling	1.8		
Lighting	0.4		
Commercial and public		14.2	11.2
Total		125.4	100%

in most of these sectors are available by better housekeeping and with essentially no change in life-style. Probably an equally large saving can be realized with minor changes that will not affect amenities to any significant degree. A reduction to less than half of the current consumption of energy is available without a total scarifice. Table 10.2 provides suggestions for each level of savings in the residential and transport sectors; similar savings are possible in the commercial and industrial sectors.

10.9   Transportation in Toroid[10]

In 1973 the U.S. Department of Commerce[11] reports that 101 million automobiles were registered in the United States. Of all family units 83 percent owned at least one car and 28 percent owned two or more. The 954 billion passenger-vehicle-miles driven resulted in 9926 miles per passenger car. In January 1974, when gasoline was 40 cents per gallon, the Department of Commerce estimated that each automobile cost $1600 per year to operate or approximately $0.16 per mile. With the increased costs of the past several years, many experienced observers estimate that it costs over $0.20 per mile to operate an automobile today.

If Toroid were a typical American city of 1 million population, one would expect it to produce over 360,000 auto registrations (excluding trucks) and an expenditure by its citizens of approximately $600 million per year on auto transport. This estimate excludes all public capital costs and all public operating costs, not all of which, by any means, are paid for by user taxes. This total provides a tempting target for cost savings through an optimum utilization of mass transit in Toroid.

Safe, efficient, fast, comfortable, reliable mass transit service within each high-density node, between the various nodes, and between each satellite community and a high-density node would result in the following:

- Effective elimination of the need for a second car in most family units.
- Significant reduction in the miles of use per private vehicle.
- Significant reduction in the proportion of private vehicles used for the journey to work.

It must be kept in mind, however, that the automobile is more than transportation for the typical American. It is a storage locker, a pickup truck, a place of privacy, a source of pleasure, and an extension of one's ego. It would be an extension of totalitarian thinking for systems analysts to decide that, since automobiles are expensive and per se "bad" and mass transit is economical and thus "good," Toroid will not provide the opportunity for choice. For public transport to contribute to the well being of Toroid's citizens and therefore to its overall success, it must be the freely chosen option. This does not mean, of course, that private vehicles need to be subsidized as they are in so many ways in present cities. They should pay their full share of pollution costs, parking costs, traffic enforcement costs, and so forth.

Given excellent public transport and full-cost charges on automobiles, it is to be expected that the private car will play a much reduced, and perhaps negligible, role in the high-density core transport in Toroid but will be of some importance in the lower-density satellite communities, for recreation, and for intercity travel.

A recent study for CEQ, HUG, and EPA[12] indicates possible significant savings in the transport sector by means of planned development. Since these estimates are based on conventional cities and incremental change, it is to be anticipated that Toroid could exceed these savings to a significant degree.

- Capital cost savings of 10 to 15 percent in street and road costs simply by controlling the rate of growth.
- A 20 to 40 percent decrease in travel times because of reduced auto use and improved circulation.

Table 10.2 *Suggested Tactics for Achieving Various Levels of Energy Savings in Residential and Transportation Sectors (Similar savings are possible in commercial and industrial sectors.)*

Sector	Energy Reduction (%)		
	10–20	20–40	40–60
1. Residential			
Heating	Adjust oil burner, clean flue, add storm windows, repair leaky hot-water taps.	Plus: Add insulation, add humidifier, lower thermostat to 70–72°. Plant conifers north of house.	Plus: Close off unused rooms, lower temperatures in bedrooms, set thermostat to 65–68°.
Cooling	Lower blinds, add awnings. Plant deciduous trees south of house.	Plus: Add dehumidifier, raise air conditioner setting to 75–78°. Paint house white.	Plus: Eliminate air conditioning except for special heat waves, set temperature at 80°. Add white roof.
Lighting	Turn off lights in unused rooms.	Plus: Reduce wattage in all lamps, substitute fluorescent lamps when possible.	Plus: Lights in only one or two rooms, minimum-wattage bulbs, no outside lights.
Appliances	Wash dishes once a day, using only full loads; ration opening refrigerator. Eliminate all gadget appliances (electric can openers, carving knife, popcorn makers, electric hair dryers, etc.)	Plus: Eliminate self-defrosting refrigerator, self-cleaning stove. Lower setting on electric hot-water heater. Use toaster oven instead of full-size oven. Add attic fan.	Plus: Substitute crock pot for oven; ration TV, stereo. Eliminate electric dishwasher, electric vacuum cleaner. Wash clothes in cold water.

Table 10.2 *(Continued)*

Sector	Energy Reduction (%)		
	10–20	20–40	40–60
2. Transportation	Have engine tune-up, use radial tires, drive 55 mph max. Shop once a week. Sell third car.	Plus: Buy smaller, lighter auto that achieves 30 mpg. Sell second car.	Plus: Use public transit in journey to work or join car pool.

- A 20 to 40 percent decrease in traffic accidents.
- Significantly lower air pollution due to the transportation sector.

None of these savings, it should be emphasized, results from the substitution of mass transit for automobiles. All are due only to properly controlled growth and intelligent design for the auto mode of transportation.

In addition to private transport for recreation and use in low-density areas, integrated transport for Toroid will consist of four major public modes. The operational requirements for each of these modes must be established as a result of several basic assumptions on the ride parameters acceptable to most citizens. These parameters are usually expressed as low cost, reliability, safety, and speed. Yet to some analysts these appear to be derived or vocalized attributes rather than basic needs. For example, take the matter of low cost. Although this is without doubt the most common of all proposed attributes, much available evidence, ignored for the most part by transportation system designers, contradicts this assumption. Consider the following:

- Public transit fares are a perennial source of controversy, it is true. A massive outcry from citizens may be expected at each incremental upward step. Most authorities would argue that there is a hard "resistance level" at a \$0.50 fare (prior "resistance levels" at \$0.05, \$0.10, and \$0.25 may be recalled). Yet the comparative work trip by private automobile costs the operator \$5 or more.[13]
- Most if not all auto owners plead disinterest in, or ignorance of, the real total costs of ownership. Vigorous disbelief may be expected at the (provable) claim that auto transport absorbs 20 to 25 percent of the *gross* income of many owners.[14]
- Many auto owners argue (and apparently believe) that driving their cars to work is cheaper than public transit.[15]
- Even if public transit fares are reduced to zero, many auto owners admit that they will not switch.[15]
- Many auto owners who claim they would switch to public transit if it were just as convenient find that they are unable to do so when it is provided. Surveys among the employees at the Cleveland airport before and after the subway was extended to the airport demonstrated a large gap (60 percent) between promises (i.e., statements of intention to switch) and actual practice.[16]
- Arguments that auto ownership is a mark of affluence and/or western materialism are demonstrably untrue. The most common symbol of "extravagance" in poor people is an expensive automobile. After

World War II western Europe moved quickly from the bicycle to the motor scooter, then to the motorcycle, then to the tiny automobile (often with three wheels), then to the larger automobile. Japan followed the same trajectory in the late 1950s. Taiwan is now midway on that trajectory, and the underdeveloped nations are anxiously seeking to begin it.

These observations are not meant to be value judgments primarily. Rather, they are intended to illustrate the claim that the common "objective" criteria for transport modes are not really the correct ones. That they are simple and measurable no one can deny, but they are not correct.

Waiting time is another incorrectly perceived parameter. It is commonly held that to be successful a public transit system must minimize waiting time. Unfortunately the solution to this problem, as expressed, is capital intensive and labor intensive. Yet ample evidence is available to show that waiting time per se is *not* the problem. Users will wait, provided that they know precisely how long they must wait. They do not trust published schedules, of course. But they will be satisfied if they have a personally addressed message from a dial-a-bus dispatcher, for example, or a direct measure of arrival time, as with a countdown clock display or moving light on a curb display. Thus, reduction of uncertainty is the correct criterion. To arrange such a display, given modern solid-state electronics, would be simple and economical.

The safety criterion is not usually correctly appreciated either. After all, public transit is already more than 10 times less risky than private automobiles on a passenger-mile basis. Starr has indicated[17] evidence to show that individuals will accept on a voluntary basis 10 times or more the risk that they will if the risk if forced on them. Thus it could be argued that concern with present safety standards in mass transit is not a concern with objective risk; rather it is an expression of the riders' objection to surrendering control.

This is not the place for a complete system analysis of urban transport, but we have said enough, it is hoped, to show that a basic value system analysis and a careful, axiologically based transport system design will be needed if public transport in Toroid is to be successful. The following partial list of criteria appears to have more validity than commonly used "objective" criteria in determining modal choice, and these items, among others, should be considered in the axiological analysis.

- *Control.* The public transit user appears to surrender control of his own destiny for a period. How can this appearance be overcome? Inexperienced transit riders display anxiety about the route the vehicle will take ("Am I on the right bus?" "Is my stop next?"). An animated display of the route and stops could be arranged inside the vehicle.

- *Privacy.* Intrusion into one's "personal space" is a common feature in public transport (crowding, pushing, shoving, etc.). How can such "personal space" be preserved? Since "personal space" is to a significant degree subjective, the solution need not necessarily be capital intensive.
- *Reduction of uncertainty.* This factor is more important than waiting time per se. Customers will wait if they know exactly how long the wait is to be. Reduction of uncertainty in waiting time may be simply a matter of displaying a "time-to-wait" clock at each station.
- *Master–servant relationship perception.* Why is the authority figure (driver, fare taker, conductor, etc.) on public transit so perceived? The waiter in a restaurant or the clerk in a store is not viewed in this way. Many potential riders do not wish to subject themselves to this situation. Suppose that the fare token could be used as a tip or a vote. Would this reverse the psychological relationship? Two slots could be arranged for the token, one whereby the rider expresses approval and the other disapproval. Merit raises could be given to popular drivers, and so on.
- *Other.*

It is possible to calculate the gross operating characteristics (speed, frequency, carrying capacity, etc.) required of the basic four kinds of public transit links for Toroid on the basis of only a few primitive, conservative assumptions.

- A median time for the work trip of 30 minutes with a range from 20 to 40 minutes.
- A maximum acceleration of ±2 miles per hour per second.
- Adjacent nodes 25 miles apart.
- A rush hour (journey to work period) lasting 1 hour.
- A satellite-to-center-of-node distance of 5 miles.
- A need for 300,000 jobs for a population of 1 million.
- Half of these in the home satellite, half of the remainder in the home central node.

Internode Transport

This will be a high-speed link (HSGT). A worker can work in his home node, of course, but some workers will wish to travel to other nodes, especially if Factoris becomes a heavy industry node. With a nodal population of 200,000 per node requiring 60,000 jobs, suppose that 30,000 persons will leave a home satellite on the journey to the central node, and 15,000 will leave each central node during the rush hour, 7000 each way. A headway of 3 minutes will permit 20 trains (platoons) on the guideway each way in 1 hour or 350 persons per car, assuming that only one car in the three-car train stops at each station. Since the rush will probably cover more than 1 hour, a 300-seat car should suffice during the rush. Smaller cars could be used during nonrush periods.

Let the typical 30-minute work trip be from one satellite to a central node and then to the adjacent central node. If 10 minutes is consumed from satellite to central node and a 2-minute wait is required for the HSGT vehicle, 18 minutes remain. Let 5 minutes be assigned to the destination node for the low-speed (moving belt) link to the workplace. Then 13 minutes remain for the 25-mile, HSGT link journey. This will require a top speed of between 120 and 150 miles per hour, not out of the question with today's technology and with well-maintained equipment.

Satellite-to-Central-Node Link

This will probably take the form of a PRT light rail or horizontal elevator. To make a 5-mile journey in 5 to 7 minutes requires a top speed of 50 to 70 miles per hour with automatic control of velocity and headway. Surprisingly, this may prove to be the most exacting technical design task of all the links, since high passenger usage will not be available except at rush hour and the design economics consequently will be difficult.

Intrasatellite Transport

The journey from home to town center may take as long as 4 minutes and cover 1 to 2 miles. Thus a 40-mile-per-hour vehicle will suffice. An automatically controlled bus may do, and "dial-a-bus" should be considered. This link does not appear to present any particular technical difficulty.

Intranode Link

Moving belts appear to present an attractive possibility for moving many persons over short distances within a central node in reasonable times. In 2 minutes a belt moving at 10 miles per hour can cover almost 600 yards or one-third of a mile. However, a 10-mile-per-hour belt provides a considerable technical challenge if it is to be safe and smooth. For several years Battelle Institute at Geneva has had under study the problem of accelerating and merging moving belts. Although the Battelle system is not completely ready for installation, early tests appear promising. This mode requires further development.

10.10   Toroid: The First Year

In Figure 10.4 is shown a gross estimate of the population growth of Toroid. It will be noted that the rate of change of growth is high throughout the first 3 years, and hence this will be a most critical period. In Figure 10.5 is shown a Gantt chart of the estimated construction effort for the project. It will be recalled that Toroid consists of six widely separated, high-density nodes interconnected by means of a high-speed ground transportation system. In Figure 10.6 we give a Gantt chart for the proposed construction effort at the first site.

Two of the high-density nodes make special claims to be the location

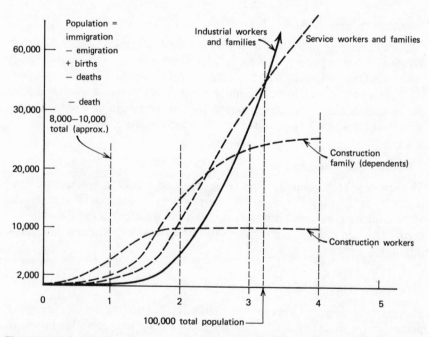

Figure 10.4   Gross population growth of Toroid for first 5 years. *Services* must be put in place for construction workers within several months of Time Zero. *Industrial* plants cannot be put into operation in less than one year on the average, then must rapidly increase production to efficient levels. *Permanent* housing for construction workers will be an early priority item.

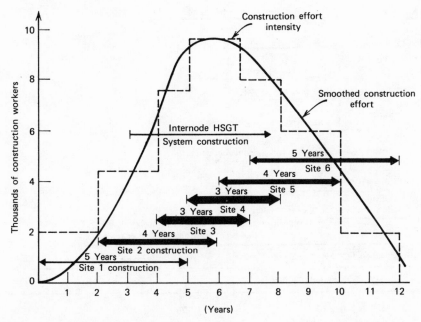

Figure 10.5   A Gantt chart of the gross construction effort for Toroid. Breadth of arrows indicate intensity of effort, that is, manpower required.

for construction initiation. In Figure 10.7 is shown an artist's conception of the six nodes linked by the HSGT system, and Figure 10.8 shows a schematic of one satellite to a high-density node. Terminus is the location for the airport that connects Toroid with the outside world. Of course, there will also be rail and interstate highway links as well and these should also be at Terminus. Thus we have in Terminus a prime candidate for construction initiation. Another early node and a possibility for the first site is Factoris. At Factoris will be located most of the export industry for Toroid, as well as the main nuclear reactor. Factoris differs from the other five nodes in its projected high-energy requirements and in its somewhat smaller permanent residential population.

A recent study by General Electric for the National Science Foundation indicates that concentration of energy-intensive activities can save approximately 20 percent of the usual cost of constructing a conventional disbursed energy grid.[18] The center of Factoris will consist primarily of industrial production, although transient and some permanent residents may be permitted to live there. Satellite residential areas might be allowed to surround Factoris, but it might be decided that to simplify industrial security and radiation safety Factoris will be totally closed except to

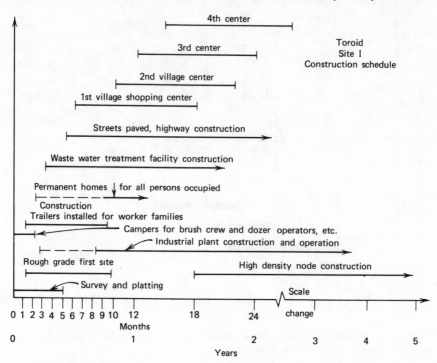

Figure 10.6 Gantt chart of construction effort at Site 1 for Toroid.

those with a need to enter. All other high-density nodes, of course, will be totally open.

From Figure 10.5 we see that construction of the HSGT system is programmed to start at year 3. Thus it would be year 4 before any HSGT service could be provided. In the meantime persons can be depended upon to utilize their private automobiles for transport. No "temporary" construction roads should be permitted to enter the interior of the ring, however, even under the argument of convenience or necessity. To do so will make the ultimate changeover to the HSGT all the harder.

It is imperative that construction begin as early as possible on the factory that will produce the industrialized housing. The first production line for housing subassemblies can and should be quite simple in order to reduce start-up time and lag in investment return. Nevertheless, this first line should be located at its permanent site so as to minimize transition difficulties. If construction is initiated on this factory at month 2, it is unlikely that finished subassemblies will be produced before month 8. Thus completed homes should begin to become available by month 9. The first units produced should be sold or leased to the factory workers

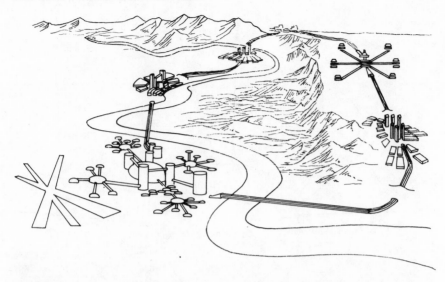

Figure 10.7 Artist's conception of Toroid, showing six high-density nodes. From the lower left, moving counterclockwise, we see Terminus, Factoris, Centralis, Colosseum, Universitas, and Senatus.

themselves. This will help motivate them to do good work and to stay on schedule.

Implications of a Ten-Year Construction Schedule

We can calculate a number of interesting implications from just a few assumptions. Some of these implications are especially pressing on the year 1 start-up process.

Assume a 10-year construction schedule for Toroid and a target population of 1 million.

Then on the average 100,000 immigrants annually must be accommodated.

Assume that each construction worker is responsible for $100,000 worth of construction annually (retail volume) and that each immigrant requires an average of $5000 worth of housing, which is the recent national average.

Then

$$\frac{\$100{,}000/\text{construction worker}}{\$5000/\text{person}} = 20 \text{ persons/construction worker}$$

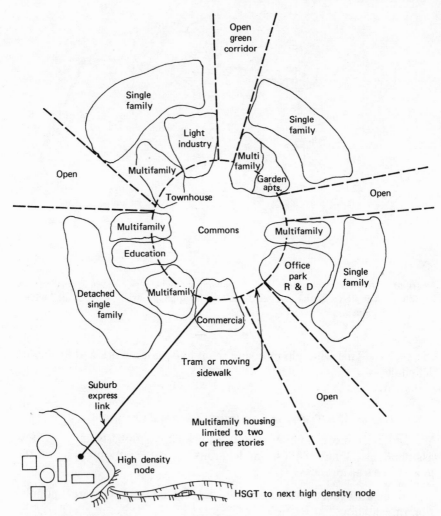

Figure 10.8 Schematic for a satellite to a high-density node.

and

$$\frac{100{,}000 \text{ persons (annual immigration rate)}}{20 \text{ persons/construction worker}} = \frac{5000 \text{ construction}}{\text{workers (housing only)}}$$

Assume that one-half of these workers are involved in transporting the industrially produced housing subassemblies, site preparation, and, finally, assembly on site, while the remaining one-half are producing the subassemblies in the factory.

Assume also a typical 100 square feet per factory worker. *Then* the housing factory will have approximately

$$100 \text{ ft}^2/\text{worker} \times 2500 \text{ workers} = 250,000 \text{ ft}^2$$

This is not a large factory, being about one city block in size. Let us double the floor area to be conservative and add auxiliary spaces.

Manufacturing area	500,000 ft²
Materials storage	500,000 ft²
Auto parking for workers	
2500 workers × 135 ft²/car =	340,000 ft²
Total	= 1,340,000 ft²

It is interesting to note that the land area devoted to workers' parking is greater than the total working space before doubling.

In the steady state, industry in Factoris should not be required to budget space so lavishly for workers' cars. If workers refuse to utilize public transport for the journey to work, the whole concept of a city organized around public transit has failed. There is no way for public transit to be economically cost effective if it is not a major component of the journey to work.

The housing factory will be reminiscent of present-day auto assembly plants in concept. It will assemble precut lumber, plastic, and metal along with electrical, plumbing, and heating components into standard subassemblies that will be capable of being assembled into a wide variety of end products. Precutting of components in anticipation of subassembly will also be done at the factory, and a number of components will be purchased from separate suppliers. Again, this is analogous to the present auto industry.

We stress this manufacturing analogy between industrialized housing and the auto industry deliberately. Not only will much of the management and production skill of the auto industry be useful in developing the industrialized housing industry, but also the latter will provide an important new business opportunity for the auto industry. Certainly most families in Toroid will continue to own an automobile, but fewer Toroid families will be multiple-car owners. This is the second major indicator for the success or failure of Toroid. For Toroid to succeed, public transit must succeed in Toroid. Yet such success bodes ill for the American auto industry as presently constituted. The auto industry represents almost 20 percent of the GNP, and it is unlikely, to say the least, that a proposed major change in transportation life-style for Americans will go unchallenged by the industry and its supporters. No one will get the modern American out of his car without a struggle. On a more objective level the nation could not afford to simply turn off auto production without concerning itself for the displacement that would result. The industrialized housing industry seems to provide a socially useful displacement. The present craft-oriented housing business is unproductive and extremely costly. If the cost of housing is reduced by industrialized techniques, price elasticity will bring many more buyers into the market and production will expand, thus absorbing the displaced auto industry. Naturally all this will be very threatening to both the present auto industry and the present housing industry. There is a great gulf between proclaiming a social goal from a safe university hideaway and achieving it in practice.[19]

Assume 4 persons per family and 100,000 immigrants yearly.

Then 25,000 housing units will be needed annually. If full-scale production is achieved by month 9, only one-quarter of a year's production is possible. However, immigration during year 1 will be well below normal.

Assume that year 1 immigration is approximately 10,000 persons, as shown in Figure 10.4.

Then

$$\frac{25,000}{4} \text{ housing units produced} \times 4 \text{ persons per family} =$$

$$25,000 \text{ persons in permanent housing } (maximum)$$

This number means that a safe cushion will be available for entering year 2.

Obviously Toroid planners could not encourage early migrant construction workers to bring with them or to purchase temporary shelter such as house trailers and then force these people to abandon their investment. To ignore this problem is to encourage squatter settlements immediately outside Toroid boundaries. During most of the first year adequate permanent housing will not be available. In month 9 the maximum housing deficiency of approximately 2000 units will exist. Even at $1000 per person for temporary shelter this means an investment of $8 million dollars (8000 persons × $1000 per person). Some of this investment, possibly even all of it, will be regained in rents. But there may be some net loss.

When will families of construction workers be encouraged to come to Toroid? In Figure 10.9 are shown two possible trajectories. In trajectory A, workers' families are discouraged until after month 9, when permanent housing produced on site first becomes available. With this trajectory more workers are on site for a given total population, and construction proceeds more rapidly. However, this trajectory will encourage the development of squatter settlements and a generally unsavory social envi-

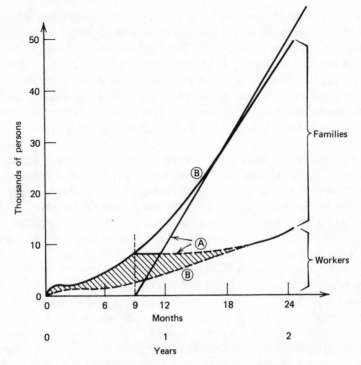

Figure 10.9   Toroid population in first 2 years.

ronment. Trajectory B, therefore, is recommended. Provision should be made from the beginning for family-type house trailer villages. Landscaping and family recreation opportunities should be part of such villages. Provision for the purchase of such trailers with guaranteed repurchase provisions could be made. Alternatively, arrangements could be made for industrialized housing companies such as National Homes, Inc., to assign a significant portion of their production to the Toroid market during year 1. This would provide permanent housing from the very beginning of Toroid. Even though transportation costs would raise prices of imported houses slightly above on-site construction, the positive social value would be great. Therefore trajectory B is strongly recommended.

10.11   Conclusion

It would be possible to analyze in much more detail the construction process of Toroid through the early years, and this was my original plan.

It was also planned to end the book with a scenario of life in Toroid some years after its completion. As interesting as this might be, however, such a scenario lies closer to science fiction than it does to systemic analysis. We have repeatedly argued that the best design is minimum design. Thus it is not the place of this system study to argue the detailed organization of villages or to speculate on the shape of individual buildings in the high-density nodes. That is the province of the architect. Thus the proposed closing scenario would imply details for which there is no present design basis.

Perhaps the most persuasive reason for not providing a speculative scenario of life in the future Toroid, however, is that a description is available of a new city that exists in reality and is similar in many of its principles to Toroid. Tapiola is a new town outside Helsinki, Finland, which has already realized in practice a number of the advantages anticipated for Toroid. Tapiola is not large, nor is it completely freestanding. Yet it is much more than a satellite or bedroom community. A garden city designed for approximately 20,000 persons, it was brought into existence in a 10-year period using entirely private capital. The creator of Tapiola, Heikki von Hertzen, has described the planning and construction of his vision.[20] He discusses frankly the problems and successes. Although von Hertzen is now aware that a population of 20,000 is not large enough, he wisely restricted the size of Tapiola to remain within available funds and to serve as an experiment. He now plans to link together a number of new towns with Helsinki in a regional plan for southern Finland. The total population of this grouping of eight nodes will be approximately 1.3 million. The growth of Helsinki will stop at 600,000 if the von Hertzen plan is adopted. Yet opposition exists for this visionary new city, just as it did concerning the original Tapiola planning.

We need not speculate over whether opposition to Toroid might arise. We can merely read the history of Tapiola. For example:

Every time you want to make an important reform or present a farsighted project you can expect to meet with stubborn conservatism and deep prejudice. Not only are authorities conservative, so are public opinion and the press. Most industrialists and businessmen think they are farsighted men of tomorrow. Among these men, in fact, the percentage of conservatives is even higher than the average of the public at large. It is hard to believe but it is true. It is such a problem that you cannot realize a new town project without finding a remedy for this obstacle.[21]

We close with this remark of von Hertzen (p. 74):

[My early work] revealed that neither those responsible for social policy nor most planners had satisfactory answers for handling Finland's planning of housing needs. People sought better and roomier dwellings, space for the young, and playgrounds for children. People wanted fresh air to breathe. They needed good surroundings and good service in residential areas. These were just as important as their dwellings. [My writings] aroused much argument, which extended over a period of five years. But the end result was nil. Those, like myself, who wanted to revitalize town planning kept hearing the same answer—that we were utopians who meant well but whose ideas could not be realized. We were also told that only experienced local civil servants and building contractors understood the seemingly iron laws of economics regarding housing and town planning. We were told that it was not possible to do anything but continue along the same old lines.

Because we knew that this argument was wrong, our only course was to prove it to be wrong. We who believed that new town planning methods could be created decided to begin building a new town ourselves.

And they did.

Notes and References

1. H. T. Odum, *Environment, Power and Society*, Wiley-Interscience, N.Y., 1971.

2. See, for example, the front page of the *Seattle Post Intelligencer* for February 17, 1971.

3. See, for example, G. B. Dantzig, T. L. Saaty, *The Compact City*, W. H. Freeman and Co., San Francisco, 1973.

4. J. D. Owens, R. G. Rivera, S. Sundararajan, N. Tamura, *DELTA Charts for the Design and Construction of a New City*, Technical Report, School of Engineering, Oakland University, Rochester, Mich., April 1973.

5. P. Blake, "Can Technology Solve the Housing Crisis?" *Atlantic Monthly*, October 1975, p. 52 et seq.

6. See, for example, D. N. Wentz, *Housing in Toroid*, Technical Report of Urban Systems Group, School of Engineering and Applied Science, University of Virginia, Charlottesville, August 1975.

7. Unfortunately, programs to rationalize the housing business have a long history of economic failure. George Pullman, founder of the Pullman Sleeping Car Company, tried in the 1880s in Pullman, Ill., and William C. Durant, the founder of General Motors, tried in Detroit before World War I. Although both were extremely successful businessmen and both possessed broad viewpoints for their times, neither was able to provide economic housing for his workers despite his best efforts. An early "New Deal" development designed to provide low-cost public housing for needy Appalachian families, located at Arthurdale, W. Va., and having the personal backing of Eleanor Roosevelt, carried cost estimates of $2000 per house. The final cost, however, was $17,000 each. This would be equivalent to a price tag of $80,000 to $100,000 in the early 1970s.

8. D. J. Rose, "Energy Policy in the U. S.," *Scientific American*, Vol. 230, No. 1 (January 1974), pp. 20–29.

9. C. Miller, *Energy Consumption in Toroid*, Technical Report of Urban Systems Group, School of Engineering and Applied Science, University of Virginia, Charlottesville, January 1976.

10. J. R. Binkley, *Transportation in Toroid,* Technical Report of Urban System Group, School of Engineering and Applied Science, University of Virginia, Charlottesville, January 1976.

11. *Statistical Abstracts of the U. S.,* Section 21, October 1974.

12. *The Costs of Sprawl,* Real Estate Research Corporation, April 1974.

13. If this is incredible to the reader, he is advised to do his own calculation. An attitude of unbelief at real costs is part of the psychological underpinning of private transport that we are attempting to explore in this section.

14. Self-deceptions such as the following are common. "I do my own repair work." "I don't need to count the cost of the garage and driveway; they came with the house." "I can't depend on public transport." "Bus lines don't run near my job." All of these statements can be true of course, but that does not reduce the real cost of operating an automobile.

15. P. M. Williams, "Low Fares and the Urban Transport Problem," *Urban Studies,* Vol. 6, No. 2 (February 1969), pp. 83–92.

16. "Survey Results, Cleveland–Hopkins Airport Access Study," Report by Cuyahoga County, Ohio Regional Planning Commission to UMTA, DOT, June 1970.

17. C. Starr, "Social Benefit versus Technological Risk," *Science,* Vol. 165, September 19, 1969, pp. 1232–1238.

18. "Assessment of Energy Parks," GPO Stock No. 038-000-00230, G. E. Report to National Science Foundation, Government Printing Office, Washington, D. C., 1975.

19. For an account of the trials and tribulations of one social systems planner who advocated industrialized housing see D. Nelkin, *The Politics of Housing Innovation,* Cornell University Press, Ithaca, N. Y., 1971.

20. H. von Hertzen, P. D. Spreiregen, *Building a New Town: Tapiola,* rev. ed., M.I.T. Press, Cambridge, 1973.

21. H. von Hertzen, *loc. cit.,* p. 180.

Author Index

Subject Index